# AFRICAN GREY PARROT

The Complete Guides on How to Take Good Care Of the African Grey Parrot

**KURTZ B LAKE**

# Table of Contents

# CHAPTER ONE

# INTRODUCTION

The African grey parrot is one of the most gifted speakme/ mimicking birds on this planet, giving it pretty a reputation amongst hen enthusiasts. Now not most effective do bird keepers love this intelligent chicken, it's one of the most recognizable species to fowl novices as well — every person is aware of the African grey parrot. This parrot is one of the oldest psitticine species saved through humans, with facts of the bird courting again to biblical instances. Understated beauty and a brainy no-nonsense attitude are what maintain this parrot at the height of popularity.

The African grey parrot's capability to talk and mimic sounds makes this medium-sized parrot a fascinating partner. African gray proprietors often report that their greys often speak in context and appear much attuned to their human's feelings. The African grey parrot is not just a talker however additionally called fantastically smart bird.

at first glance, the African gray is a medium-sized, dusty-searching gray bird, almost pigeon-like — however similarly investigation well-known shows a bright crimson tail, wise orange eyes, and a beautiful scalloped sample to its plumage.

# CHAPTER TWO

# AFRICAN GREY PARROT DWELLINGS

African gray parrots typically inhabit savannas, coastal mangroves, forest and edges of woodland clearings of their West and central Africa variety. even though the larger of the African gray subspecies is known as the Congo African grey, this chicken surely has a miles wider herbal range in Africa, such as the southeastern Ivory Coast, Kenya, and Tanzania. The Timneh African grey is observed in a smaller place along the western fringe of the Ivory Coast and through southern Guinea. Their eating regimen within the wild consists commonly of palm nuts, seeds, end result, and leafy count number.

# CHAPTER THREE

# HOW TO TAKE GOOD CARE AND FEED YOUR AFRICAN GREY PARROT

There's a purpose why the African grey is frequently taken into consideration the poster fowl for parrot intelligence — not only is this bird inclined to amass a large vocabulary, African greys also display a flair for recognizing the meaning of words and phrases.

African greys need masses of toys that project their intelligence, consisting of foraging and puzzle toys. This complete food blends a stability of grains, seeds, and other nutrients within the form of a berry. Due to the fact the grains and seeds are often whole and shaped right into a berry shape, it encourages African greys to hold, nibble, or even play with the Nutri-Berries. This mimics the foraging that African greys do within the wild.

African greys seem mainly stricken by pressure and commotion in their environment and can be positioned extra secure with the aid of putting one corner of the cage towards a wall rather than within the middle of a room.

African grey parrots are extra liable to deficiency in nutrition-A/beta-carotene, and consequently benefit from eating veggies excessive in beta-carotene, together with cooked candy potato and fresh kale. Nutrition-D deficiency is every other subject, in particular for greys on a terrible weight-reduction plan. Offering a balanced, pelleted diet, such as Nutri-Berries, for the main weight loss program of an African grey enables save you diet and mineral deficiencies. A gray that consumes a pelleted food regimen typically does now not need nutrition dietary supplements added to its meals.

Due to the fact they are so smart, African grey parrots form very robust bonds with their proprietors and may be pretty emotionally needy. Due to this trait, they do first-class with owners who can dedicate enough time to dealing with and socializing with them day by day. Additionally, African grey parrots want plenty of exercise to preserve their strong muscle mass toned and preserve an adequate physical situation. Which means they ought to be able to spend numerous hours in line with day outside in their cages, gambling in supervised, "parrot evidence" areas.

# CHAPTER FOUR

# BEHAVIOR OF AFRICAN GREY PARROT

Most fowl keepers agree with that simplest an experienced bird enthusiast have to maintain a gray. They are complex parrots, highly sensitive, and more than a touch traumatic. They're additionally fascinating and splendid, however this fit of sensitivity and brains can lead to behavioral troubles. They are creatures of addiction, and even a small alternate in recurring can make a sensitive grey sad. They are susceptible to plucking and chewing their feathers, among different horrific behavior. Anecdotally, the TAG has a hardier mind-set and may be better for families with plenty of human beings coming and going. The CAG prefers a touch much less chaos.

African greys are social parrots that need a number of hands-on times, however, they aren't "cuddlebugs." they will tolerate some head scratching and a bit little bit of petting, however they do now not recognize excessive physical contact, though some individuals don't mind a bit snuggling. Each bird has person tastes and preferences. A grey can also grow to be a "one man or woman chook," even supposing each member of the family socializes with it from the start.

Speech & Sound

An awful lot of the gray's enchantment comes from its speaking capacity. it's far among the great talkers within the parrot circle of relatives, able to repeat words and terms after listening to them simply a few times. This hen reaches full talking capacity around 12 months of age, and maximum people grow to be capable mimics a lot earlier.

Now not best will a grey expand an extraordinary vocabulary, research has shown that this species can come to recognize what it's saying. But just due to the fact greys are smart and might pick to speak in preference to scream, it's a mistake to trust that they aren't noisy. They aren't as loud or persistent as a number of the South American species, however they may analyze household sounds and use them tirelessly to the dismay of guardians.

## Health conditions

African greys are particularly susceptible to feather picking, calcium deficiency, nutrition-A and diet-D deficiency, respiratory contamination, psittacosis and psittacine beak and feather sickness (PBFD).

# CHAPTER FIVE

# TYPES OF AFRICAN GREY PARROT

There may be more than one type.

Even as all styles of African gray parrots look similar, there are two distinct kinds and multiple lesser-recognised subspecies of this beloved bird. The most popular and commonplace is the Congo African gray. The Congo African gray is the largest of the African grey parrots, wearing a lighter grey coloration in its plumage, and a solid black beak.

The Timneh African gray is slightly smaller than the Congo, and its feathers are darker in coloration. Another defining characteristic of the Timneh gray is that it has a horn-colored upper mandible as opposed to a black one. Notwithstanding their differences, each of these kinds of African grey parrots makes outstanding pets, and each are equally wise. Upper mandible instead of a black  one. Regardless of their differences, both of those varieties of African grey parrots make excellent pets, and both are similarly wise.

They can live for a completely long time

African gray parrots have been recognized to live for as much as 80 years in captivity, so it is imperative that those who undertake them can decide to an entire life of residing with a chicken. African gray parrots are too emotionally touchy with a purpose to deal with being bounced from proprietor to owner, however regrettably a lot of them do have several homes at some stage in their lifetimes because humans rush into adopting them without absolutely thinking it through. you could help positioned an cease to situations like those by means of assisting to educate human beings about African grey ownership, and by making sure that you set an awesome instance for fowl owners who might be inquisitive about adopting any such parrot.

And also, African grey parrot can relate to the problems of maintaining a young child occupied, so it's now not a stretch to mention that preserving a highly wise hen from getting bored can be comparable. African gray parrots want masses of mental stimulation to live satisfied and healthy, so that they need to be supplied with a variety of toys and other ways to exercising their minds. Otherwise, they could hotel to unfavorable behavior and broaden unsightly conduct that could require professional intervention.

# CHAPTER SIX

# WHAT MAKES AFRICAN GREY PARROTS SO INTELLIGENT

African grey parrot are so clever because their brains are very just like primate brain. Parrots have a large location that acts as an information superhighway among the 2 predominant areas of the mind.

If you've lived or labored with parrots, then you recognize first-hand that they're pretty intelligent. Parrots demonstrate state-of-the-art hassle fixing skills, they are able to speak their goals, they are able to rely, upload and subtract, and remarkably, they even recognize the concept of zero. Other studies of cockatoos have installed that they make and use their own gear. In the course of the animal nation, parrots' cognitive competencies and highbrow capabilities are simplest matched by way of corvids and primates.

In keeping with a latest study, a team of neuroscientists in Canada have recognized the mind region chargeable for parrots' exceptional intelligence. This neural circuit is just like that found in primates, along with human beings, and is the supply of their intelligence.

"An area of the mind that performs a first-rate position in primate intelligence is called the pontine nuclei." In primates (which of course, consists of people), the pontine nuclei transmit records among the cortex, which governs thinking, information processing and different higher cognitive functions, and the cerebellum, which regulates motor capabilities, coordination and balance. Collectively, these mind structures are the supply for complicated capabilities among human beings and other apes.

"This shape transfers facts among the two largest regions of the brain, the cortex and cerebellum, which allows for higher-order processing and extra sophisticated conduct.

THE END

www.ingramcontent.com/pod-product-compliance
Lightning Source LLC
Chambersburg PA
CBHW072145150726
48002CB00004B/1642